The Pals' Playtime

Graphic Novel 1

Written by Christine Hjorth

Illustrated by Belen Roldan

Go to Decodables.com for more information, products, and contact information to schedule an author visit.

IMPORTANT NOTE:

HOW TO READ AN ALIGNED DECODABLE

Aligned Decodables are set up a little different than a regular picture book. In these books the text is on the righthand side of the book, and the picture that matches that text is on the next page (instead of the text and picture being side by side). This is so the readers read the text, then turn the page to confirm meaning of what they read and build engagement and enjoyment!

Chapter 1
__Consonants__: f, x, h, d, s, n, t, b, g, v, r, m, p, y
__Short Vowels__: a, o, i, u, e
__High-Frequency Words__: the, no, ha

Chapter 2 – Add:
__Letter Patterns__: All Consonants, Double Consonants, K sound spelled "CK"
__High-Frequency Words__: what, to, with, find
__Word Ending__: -s

A "double consonant" is when a consonant is doubled, but only makes one sounds. For example, SS, LL, FF.

Chapter 3 – Add:
__Letter Patterns__: Digraphs, Beginning and Ending Blends, CV words
__High-Frequency Words__: you, out

A "digraph" is two letters that when put together make a whole new sound. For example, SH, TH, CH, WH.

A "blend" is two consonants that are next to each other and the sounds blend together. For example, beginning blends BL, CR, SW or ending blends NK, NG, FT.

A "CV" word is a consonant-vowel word, where the vowel is long. For example, me, be, he.

Chapter 4 – Add:
__Letter Patterns__: R-Controlled Vowels, Silent E
__Word Ending__: -ed, -ing, -es
__High-Frequency Words__: do, one, party

An "r-controlled vowel" is when the vowel is next to an "r", and the "r" makes it say a new sound. For example, OR, AR, IR, UR, ER.

A "Silent E" word is when a word has a vowel-consonant-E letter pattern at the end of the word. The "e" is silent and makes the vowel in the word long. For example, bike, hole, or stone.

One

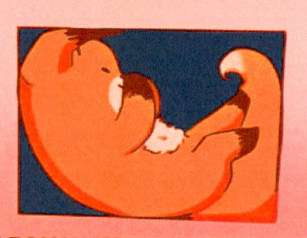

FOX

HID

Before you read the first story, you need to learn these letter sounds and words!
You can do it!

Consonants f, x, h, d, s, n, t, b, g, v, r, m, p, y

Short Vowels: a, o, i, u, e

High-Frequency Words: the, no, ha

Fox hid.

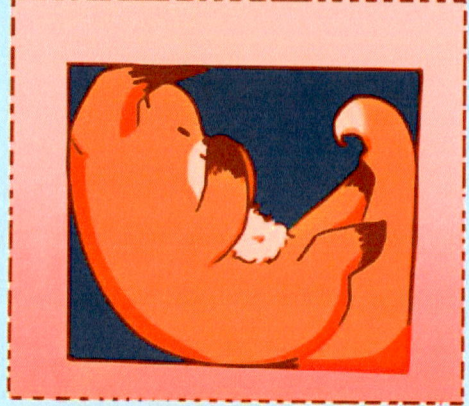

Is Fox in the tub?

Is Fox in the bed?

8

Is Fox in the van?

No, it is Ram.

Fox?

Fox!

Is Fox in the box?

Yes!
Fox and Pig
hug!

Fox!

<u>Comprehension Questions</u>

1. Name one place Pig looked for Fox.
2. Do you think it was a good hiding place? Why or why not?
3. Where do you like to hide when you play hide and seek?

CONGRATULATIONS!

You read the first story!

Before you move on to the next story, you need to learn these additional letter patterns and words!

You can do it!

Letter Patterns: All Consonants, Double Consonants, K sound spelled "CK"
High-Frequency Words: what, to, with, find
Word Ending: -s

If you are looking for more practice like this first story, check out these stories found in other Stages books!

Stages: Dogs

One

DOGS!

Before you read the first story, you need to learn these letter sounds and words!
You can do it!

Consonants: d, g, s, f, n, c, m, h, t, j, b, w
Short Vowels: a, o, i, u
High-Frequency Words: do, the, be

Stages: Pat and Tim Fun Times

One

Pat and Tim

Before you read this story, you need to learn these letter sounds and words!
You can do it!
Consonants: t, s, p, m, r, c, h, n, j, g, f, v, z
Short Vowels: a, i, o

Stages: Spiders

One

On a Web

Before you read this story, you need to learn these letter patterns and words!
You can do it!
Consonants: t, s, n, l, g, h, p, c, b, w, r, d
Short Vowels: a, e, i, o, u
High-Frequency Words: the
Word Ending: -s

Stages: Pat and Tim Fun Times

Two

The Mad Pals

Phonics Skills
t, s, p, m, r, c, h, n, j, g, f, v, z, d, w, x, b
Short Vowels a, e, i, o
High-Frequency Words
the, to

Two

The Box

Phonics Skills
All Consonants, All Short Vowels,
Double Consonants, -CK,
Word Ending -s
High-Frequency Words
find, the, no, to, with, what

Fox and Pig find a box.

What is in it?

Fox hits the box.

No luck.

Fox will pass the box to Pig.

Pig has the box.

Pig kicks the box.

No luck.

KICK!

Pig will pass the box to Ram.

Ram has the box.

Ram rams the box.

No luck.

Ram will pass the box to Dog.

Dog has the box.

Dog licks the box.

"No Dog!"

yell the pals.

NO DOG!

Dog will
pass the
box to
Duck.

Pass!

Duck has the box.

Duck fans the box.

No luck.

Hmm...a box?

Fan! Fan!
Fan!
Fan!
Fan!
Fan!

Duck will pass the box to Cat.

Cat has the box.

Cat hits the

box with a bat.

No luck.

BAM!

Cat will pass the box to Rat.

Rat taps the

lock on the box.

POP!

Rat did it!

The box is full of gum!
Yum!

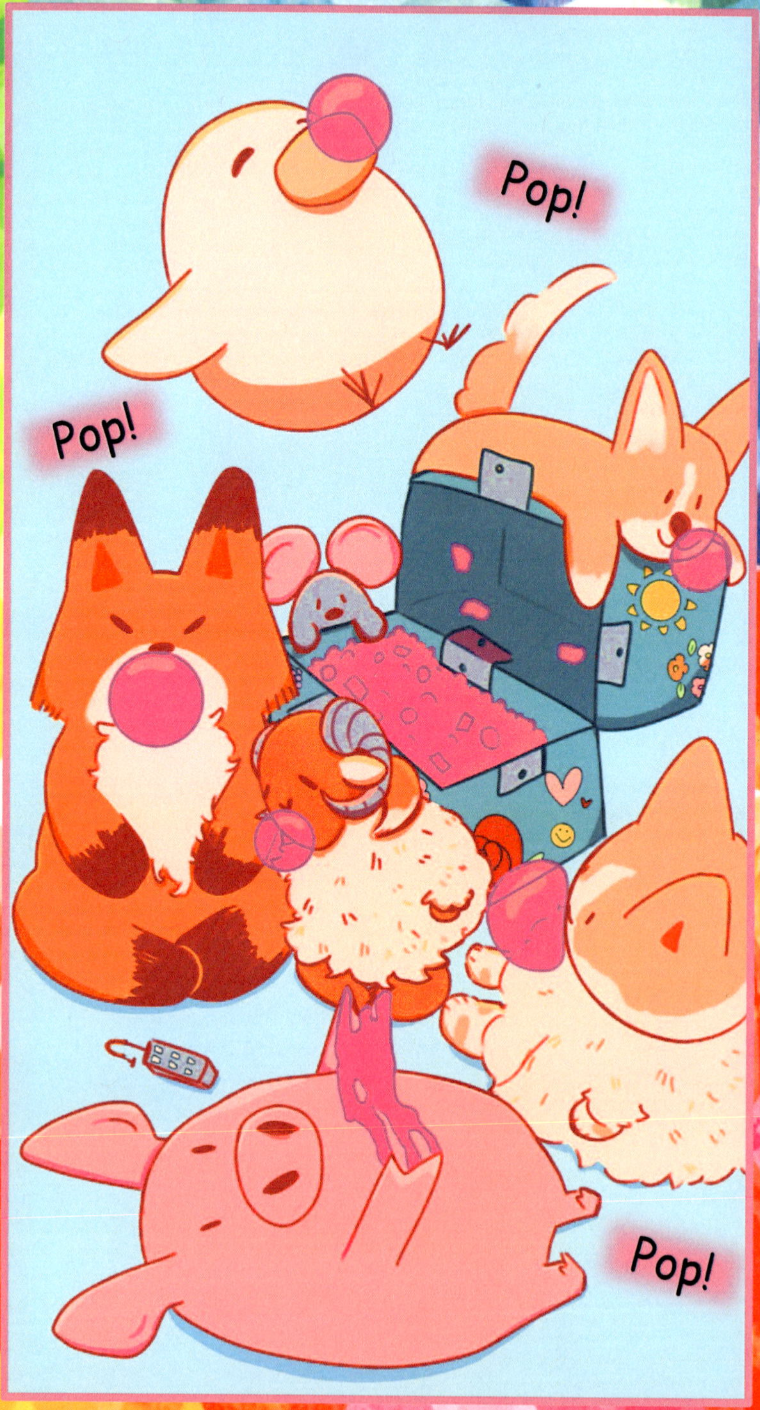
Pop!
Pop!
Pop!

Comprehension Questions

1. A "verb" is an action word. There are many different verbs in this story. Can you find at least ten?
2. How did the pals get the box open, and what was in it?
3. Tell me about a time you solved a problem.

CONGRATULATIONS!

You read the second story!

Before you move on to the next story, you need to learn these additional letter patterns and words!

You can do it!

Letter Patterns: Digraphs, Beginning and Ending Blends, CV Words
High-Frequency Words: you, out

If you are looking for more practice like this second story, check out these stories found in other Stages books!

Stages: Pat and Tim
Fun Times

Stages: Spiders

Stages: Dogs

Three STUCK!

Phonics Skills

All Consonants, Short Vowels, -CK,
Double Consonants, Blends, Digraphs,
CV Words, Word Ending -s

High-Frequency Words

to, you, out

Yuck!
Pig is up to his
chin in mud.
He is stuck.

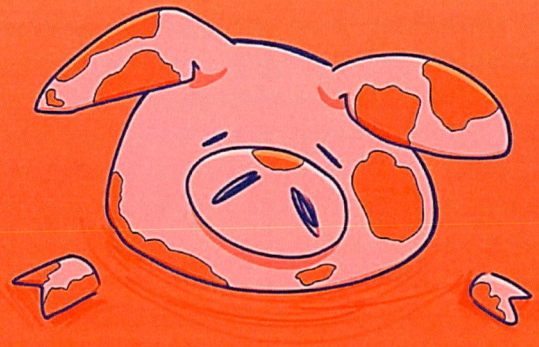

"Fox! Can you help me?"
calls Pig.
"Yes!" Fox yips back.

Fox sprints and finds Duck.
She has thin sticks.
"Duck, can you help?" Fox asks.
Duck quacks, "Yes!"

Fox and Duck dash
and find Dog.
He has strings.
"Can you help us,
Dog?" asks Fox and
Duck.
Dog nods.

48

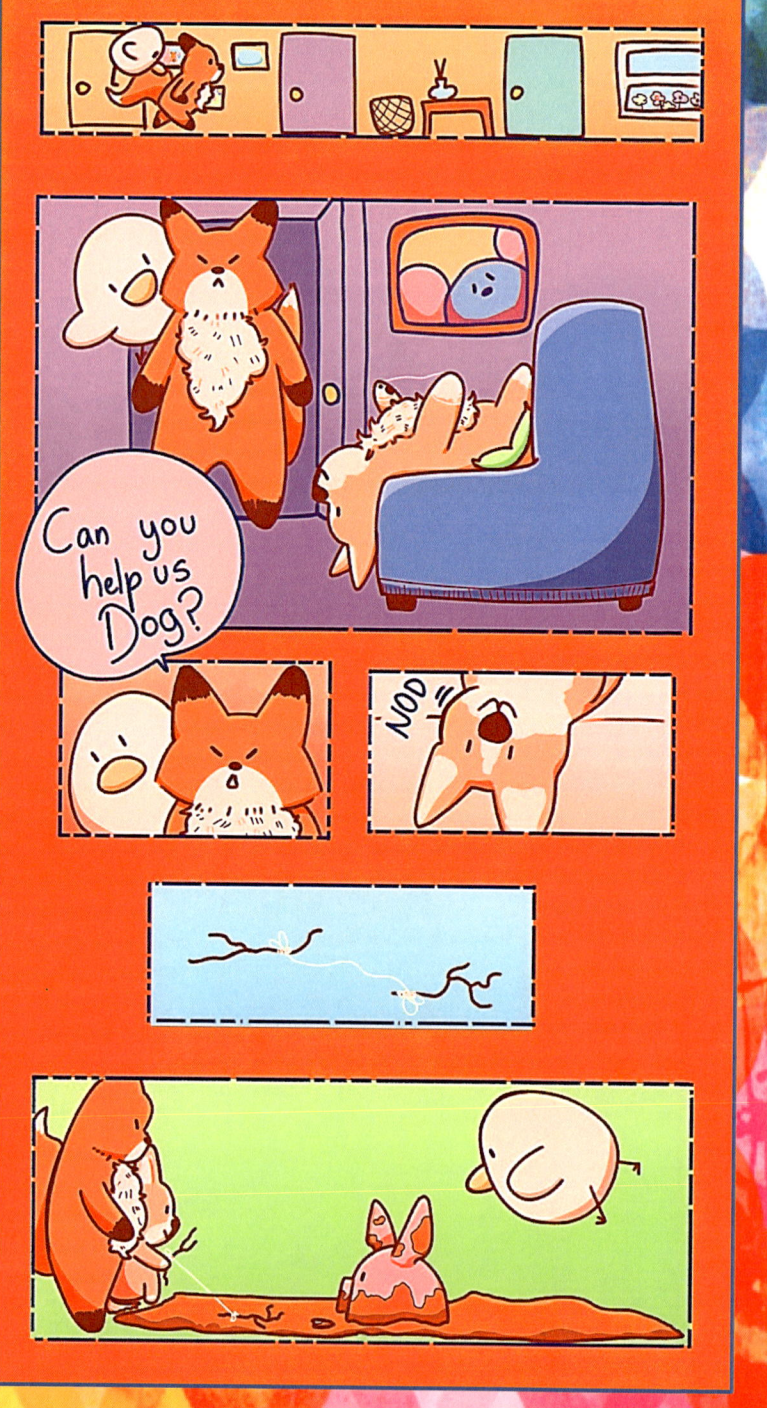

Fox, Duck, and Dog rush and find Ram. He has a club. "Ram, can you help us?" ask the pals. Ram thinks, then grunts, "Yes!"

The pals cast the end out to Pig.

Pig cannot get it.
Duck will help!

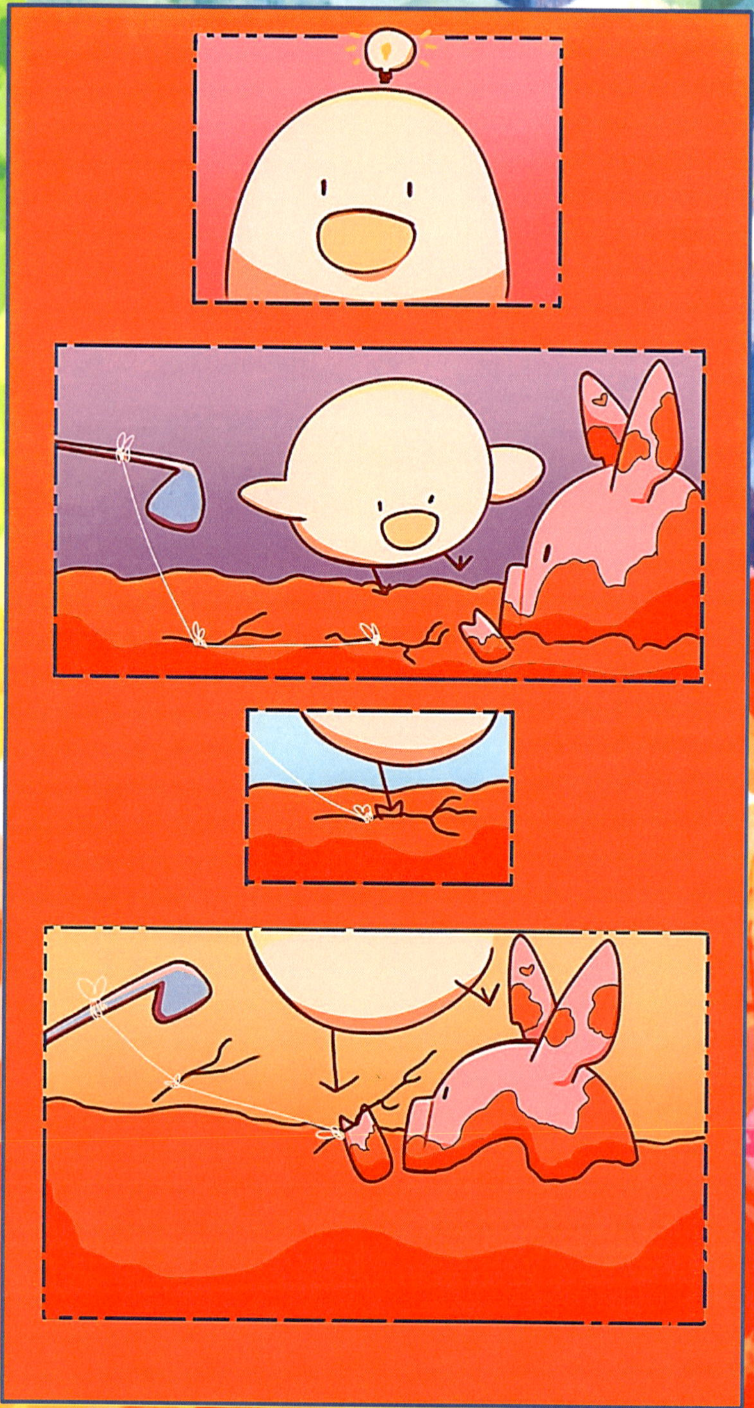

The pals tug! Pig pops out of the mud!

Pig hops back in!

Comprehension Questions

1. What was the problem in this story? What was the solution?
2. In this story, the pals work together to solve a problem. Tell me about a time when you worked together with someone.

CONGRATULATIONS!

You read the third story!

Before you move on to the next story, you need to learn these additional letter patterns and words!

You can do it!

Letter Patterns: R-Controlled Vowels, Silent E
Word Ending: -ed, -ing, -es
High-Frequency Words: do, one, party

If you are looking for more practice like this third story, check out these stories found in other Stages books!

Stages: Dogs

Three YOU AND YOUR DOG

Phonics Skills
Consonants, Short Vowels, Blends,
Double Consonants, Digraphs,
Silent E and KN-

High-Frequency Words
your, do, have, her, to, of, you

Stages: Pat and Tim Fun Times

Four FLAGS!

Phonics Skills
All Consonants, Short Vowels, Double
Consonants, Beginning and Ending
Blends, Digraphs, Word Ending -s
High-Frequency Words
he, for, make, to, they, see, likes

Stages: Spiders

Three

Kinds of Spiders

Phonics Skills
Consonants, Short Vowels,
Blends, Digraphs, Silent E,
Double Consonants,
Word Endings -s, -ing
High-Frequency Words
do, they, food, look, by, to, or

Four

Dress-Up Time

Phonics skills
All Consonants, Short Vowels, Double Consonants, Blends, Digraphs, R-Controlled Vowels, CV Words, Silent E, Word Endings -s, -ed, -ing, -es
High-Frequency Words
to, do, you, one, party

The pals are going to a costume party! The best costume will win a prize. What will the pals dress up as?

Pig puts on a black top hat and a long red cape. He has a wand in his hand and he waves it. What do you think he is dressed as?

Fox puts on fake wire glasses, a white lab coat, and black pants. He holds a chart. He taps the chart with his pen.

What do you think he is dressed as?

Duck straps a fin to her back. She bites a fake fish. She slides back and forth across the grass on a skate.

What do you think she is dressed as?

Cat tapes pinecones to her shirt. She holds branches in her hands and waves her arms.

What do you think she is dressed as?

Ram puts on overalls and a red shirt. He holds a pitch fork, that is not sharp, in one hand. He holds a corn cob in the other hand.

What do think he is dressed as?

Rat has on a pin-striped shirt with no collar. He holds a bat in one hand. With the other hand, he tosses a ball up and catches it.

What you do think he is dressed as?

Dog enters the party with one pink sock, one orange sock, one mustard sock, and one lime sock. He has a pack full of blocks on his back and a lamp shade as a hat.

Comprehension Questions

1. An "adjective" is a word that describes something. There are many adjectives in this story. Can you find at least ten?

2. The story doesn't say who won the costume contest. Who do you think would have won?

3. Have you ever dressed in a costume? What was it?

CONGRATULATIONS!

You read the fourth story!

If you are looking for more practice like this fourth story, check out these stories found in other Stages books!

Stages: Spiders

Stages: Dogs

www.ingramcontent.com/pod-product-compliance
Lightning Source LLC
Chambersburg PA
CBRC090837120626
46551CB00007B/685